FAMILIES AROUND THE WORLD

A family from
IRAQ

John King

RSVP
RAINTREE
STECK-VAUGHN
PUBLISHERS
The Steck-Vaughn Company

Austin, Texas

FAMILIES AROUND THE WORLD

A family from **BOSNIA**

A family from **BRAZIL**

A family from **CHINA**

A family from **ETHIOPIA**

A family from **GERMANY**

A family from **GUATEMALA**

A family from **IRAQ**

A family from **JAPAN**

A family from **SOUTH AFRICA**

A family from **VIETNAM**

Abed Ali and his family are members of Saddam Hussein's Baath Party. The Saleh-Ali family was chosen to be in this book by the Iraqi government.

Cover: The Saleh-Ali family outside its home with all its possessions
Title page: Abed and Alia with their five children
Contents page: The memorial to Iraqi people who died in the wars between Iraq and Iran and in the Gulf War

Picture Acknowledgments: All the photographs in this book were taken by Alexandra Boulat.
The photographs were supplied by Material World/Impact Photos and were first published by
Sierra Club Books in 1994 © Copyright Alexandra Boulat/Material World.
The map artwork on page 4 is produced by Peter Bull.

Published by Raintree Steck-Vaughn Publishers, an imprint of Steck-Vaughn Company

Printed in Italy. Bound in the United States.
1 2 3 4 5 6 7 8 9 0 02 01 00 99 98

Library of Congress Cataloging-in-Publication Data
King, John.
A family from Iraq / John King.
p. cm.—(Families around the world)
Includes bibliographical references and index.
Summary: Describes the activities of an extended family living on the outskirts of Baghdad, the capital of Iraq, providing brief information about this country's daily life and customs.
ISBN 0-8172-4904-4
1. Iraq—Social life and customs—Juvenile literature.
2. Family—Iraq—Juvenile literature.
[1.Family life—Iraq. 2. Iraq—Social life and customs.]
I. Title. II. Series: Families around the world.
DS70.7.K48   1998
306.85'09567—dc21   97-15578

Contents

Introduction	4	Spare Time	24
Meet the Family	6	The Future	28
A Home in Iraq	8	Pronunciation Guide	30
Food and Cooking	12	Glossary	31
Work	18	Books to Read	31
School and Play	22	Index	32

 # Introduction

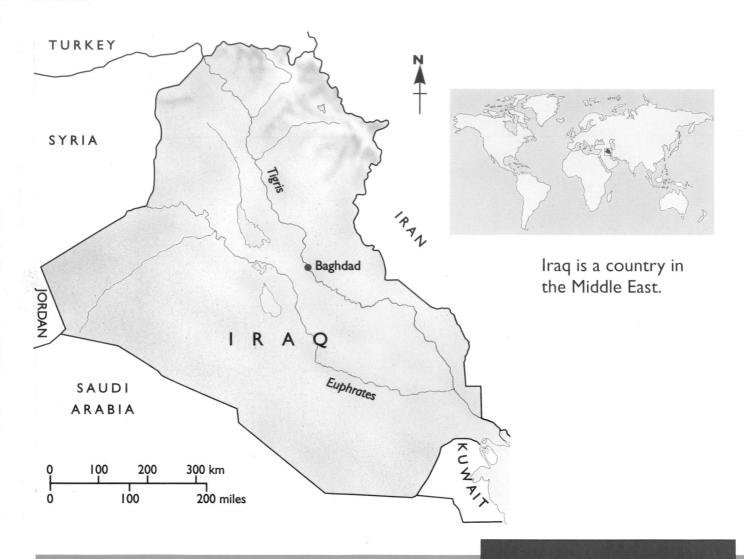

TURKEY

SYRIA

Tigris

IRAN

• Baghdad

JORDAN

I R A Q

Euphrates

SAUDI
ARABIA

N

KUWAIT

0	100	200	300 km
0		100	200 miles

Iraq is a country in
the Middle East.

REPUBLIC OF IRAQ

Capital city:	Baghdad
Size:	169,250 sq. mi. (438,320 sq. km)
Number of people:	19,500,000
Main language:	Arabic
People:	Arab 79%, Kurdish 16%, Turkish 2%, Persian 3%.
Religion:	Mainly Muslim
Currency:	Iraqi Dinar

THE SALEH-ALI FAMILY

Size of family:	11, living in two houses
Size of homes:	Both 2,150 sq. ft. (200 sq. m)
Workweek:	Average: 42 hours
Most valuable possessions:	Abed: Family and television Alia: Jewelry and children Hala: Baghdad Game
Income per person:	$1,940 each year

The Saleh-Ali family is an ordinary Iraqi family. They have put everything that they own outside their home so that this photograph could be taken.

Meet the Family

Saleh household:
1 Mahdi, father, 74
2 Shaïmaa, mother, 59
3 Amira, daughter, 34
4 Falah, son, 21

Ali household:
5 Alia, Saleh family's eldest daughter, 42
6 Abed, Alia's husband, 45
7 Wasan, daughter, 19
8 Sahar, daughter, 17
9 Hala, daughter, 12
10 Ahmad, son, 7
11 Suher, daughter, 18 months

AFTER THE WAR

Iraq is ruled by President Saddam Hussein. In 1990 his army invaded Kuwait. The United Nations punished Iraq by preventing it from selling oil and buying goods from outside the country. This means that life for many of the people of Iraq has been difficult.

The Saleh-Ali family lives in two houses on the outskirts of Baghdad, the capital city of Iraq. Mahdi and Shaïmaa live with two of their children, Amira and Falah, in the house shown in the picture on page 5. Their eldest daughter, Alia, lives with her husband, Abed, and their five children in another house nearby.

"It's fun having a large family. There is always someone to play with."
—Hala

A Home in Iraq

Baghdad is very hot in the summer. Roof terraces can be cool places to sit in the evenings.

A FULL HOUSE

Iraqi families often have many children. Grown-up sons and daughters sometimes live very near their parents or share a house with them.

The family's houses are built of brick covered with cement. The Saleh-Ali family owns both of their houses. Shaïmaa and Mahdi bought their house thirteen years ago. Abed and Alia live in the house where Abed was born. Abed's house has been in his family for two generations.

8

A Room for Everything

There are six rooms in both houses. Each house has a special living room with chairs, a table, and sofas where visitors sit on special occasions. There is also a living room for everyday use, and each house has a kitchen. The bedrooms are upstairs, and the living rooms and the kitchen are on the ground floor.

Hala always sits at the small table in the living room to do her homework.

"I love my clothes and I like to be able to look good if I go out in the evening."
—Amira

Amira has her own bedroom. She likes to keep it private and locks the door every day.

Decorations

Inside each house, the walls are painted in white or in plain colors. In the rooms, there are pictures of places in Iraq and of President Saddam Hussein. The furniture is very plain.

In the kitchen there is a stove that runs on bottled gas. Each kitchen also has a freezer and a refrigerator.

"I love to be in my kitchen, where everything is exactly how I want it to be."—*Shaïmaa*

Food and Cooking

Shaïmaa loves to cook for her family.

KUBBA

Kubba is a typical Iraqi dish. Shells made of a mixture of wheat and minced meat are filled with more meat, onions, spices, and nuts. The *kubba* are then fried and served with vegetables or yogurt. *Kubba* take a long time to make, but they are very good to eat!

A meal made by Shaïmaa for her family usually includes vegetables, potatoes, salad, lemons, and bread. The family usually eats meals that they make at home, although they can buy kebabs and other food at shops and restaurants.

Tasty Kebabs

Since the Gulf War, there have been shortages of some food. Now the family only eats meat twice a week, usually served as kebabs, or *kubba*.

Shaïmaa usually sits on the floor in her house to cook in the old-fashioned way. Her daughter, Alia, stands up to cook.

Shopping

The family spends a lot of money on food. Prices are high and often go up, although the government tries to keep them down. It is traditional in Iraq for men to buy the food. Mahdi has always been proud of his ability to buy good vegetables or a tasty piece of meat. But this tradition is changing. Mahdi's daughters, Alia and Amira, like to shop and choose food.

Street vendors such as this one in the center of Baghdad offer food for sale to passersby.

A Good Breakfast

For breakfast, the family always has tea with milk, and cheese, bread, eggs, and potatoes. When Hala and Ahmad come home from school, they are hungry and usually have a snack. A typical midday meal for the children is vegetables, eggs, and sometimes cooked chicken rolled up in a pancake.

Shaïmaa always makes a tasty yogurt drink to go with spicy food.

Eating Together

The Saleh-Ali family eats together on Friday evenings, on festival days, and whenever there is a special reason to celebrate. The whole family likes being together because it is a good time to share family news.

"The family loves my cooking. Everyone says that they would rather eat at home than at a restaurant."—*Shaïmaa*

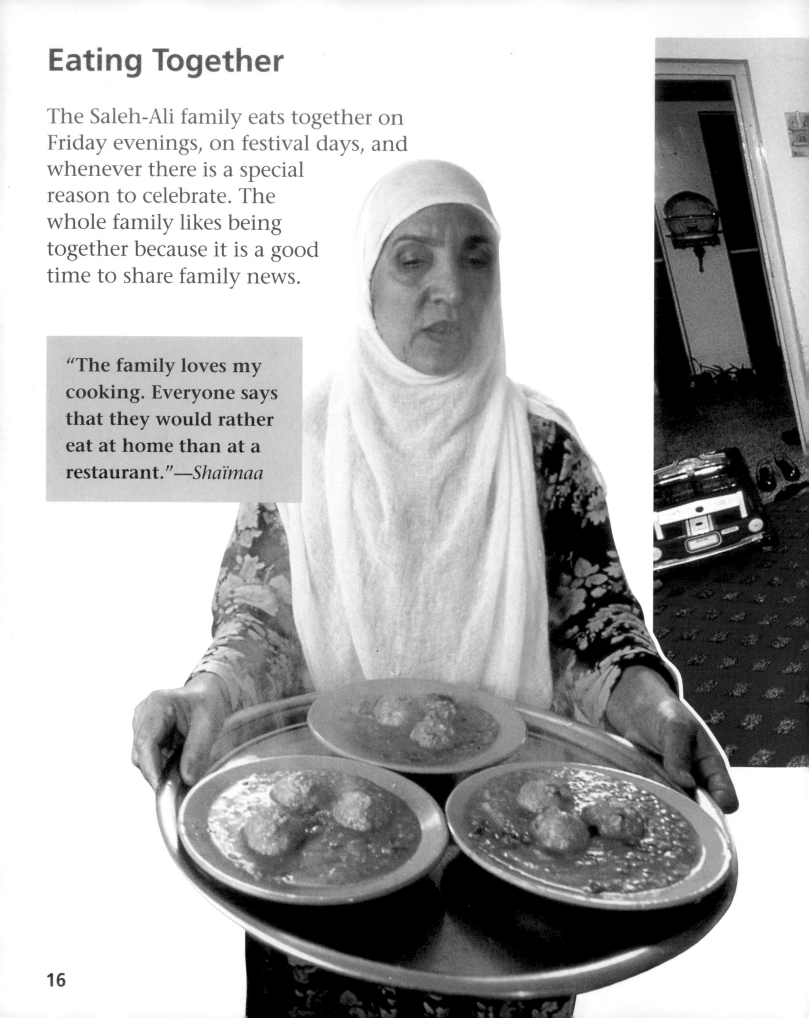

Food is an important part of family life in Iraq, just as it is in other Arab countries. The family likes to eat at home but sometimes enjoys food from a restaurant. Iraqi families spend a lot of time together, and big family meals are special occasions.

To eat, everyone sits around a mat on the floor of the living room.

17

Working Hard

When Mahdi was younger, he worked in the oil industry.

WOMEN AT WORK

Iraq is different than some other Arab countries, where women are not allowed to have jobs. Many women work in Iraq. The jobs that women do are very important for the country and for the incomes of Iraqi families.

Mahdi is 74 years old and has retired. He spent most of his working life building oil pipelines. Mahdi also worked abroad in Libya and in Sri Lanka.

"There are no new cars in Iraq, but I look after this one well. It gets me to the office, and the whole family likes to go out for drives in it on the weekend."—*Abed*

Abed has a job in an office, where he is a civilian worker for the Iraqi army. During the week, Abed drives Alia to work on his way to his office. Alia works as a teacher at a primary school.

Abed is ready to set off for work in his car.

When work at the office or the shop is over, there are still dishes to be done.

Wasan and her aunt Amira both work in a shop at Baghdad Airport. They work there every day except Friday, from eight o'clock in the morning until three o'clock in the afternoon. It is hard work, especially when there are lots of customers. At the end of the day, Wasan and Amira are usually tired because they have spent most of the day on their feet.

Falah works hard as a student. He is learning to be a musician at the Baghdad Academy of Music. Falah would like to earn his living in music. The instrument he plays is called an *oudh*. It is a traditional instrument in Arab countries and is shaped a little like a guitar. Classical and popular music can be played on it. A good *oudh* is expensive, so Falah takes good care of his.

Falah plays a melody on his *oudh* for his friends.

School and Play

Hala (in the middle of the group) is at the top of her class in school.

Studying Hard

Hala and Ahmad work hard at school. They both hope to get good jobs one day. The local school is open from seven o'clock in the morning until three o'clock in the afternoon. But Hala and Ahmad spend only three hours there each day. There aren't enough teachers for them to spend the whole day in school.

RELIGION AT SCHOOL

In Iraq, most people are Muslims. Studying religion is a very important part of the school day. The children begin to learn about Islam when they are very young.

Playtime

After school, Ahmad loves to play soccer with his friends. His favorite toy is his plastic soccer ball. But he also plays with his baby sister, Suher.

22

"When I study the Koran, our holy book, I wear gloves to keep the pages clean."—*Ahmad*

Spare Time

The whole family enjoys watching television in its spare time. Ahmad likes the soccer games best.

Watching television

The family spends a lot of time together. In the evenings they like to watch television. There is a program with popular Arabic music each evening that Wasan and Sahar like to watch. At nine o'clock each evening Abed watches the news.

Vacations

For their vacations, the Saleh-Ali family sometimes visits a little country house that it owns outside Baghdad. Hala and Ahmad enjoy sleeping in strange beds and playing in a different garden. The family can't go farther away at the moment because it would be too expensive.

Abed and Ahmad often watch television together.

"I wear a shirt and trousers to go to the office, but during my spare time I like to wear traditional Iraqi clothes."—*Abed*

The family often enjoys a stroll together.

Often the family visits a special place, such as a historic mosque. They sometimes go out into the countryside in the car and then go for a walk or have a picnic. Sometimes Abed goes to a café to meet his friends.

A TIME TO PRAY

Religion is very important in Iraq. On Fridays the men go to the mosque to pray, but the women usually pray at home.

Religion

The Saleh-Ali family is Muslim. They have texts from the Koran on the walls. Shaïmaa is the only member of the family who wears the traditional Islamic scarf to cover her head.

"I pray in the living room of my house, five times a day."—*Shaïmaa*

The Future

The Saleh-Ali family hopes for a better future. Falah wants to succeed with his music. Hala is doing well at school, and her parents hope she will have a good career. Ahmad would like to be a good soccer player for Iraq.

A BETTER FUTURE

Many thousands of Iraqi men and women have died in wars since 1980. The Gulf War is still fresh in many people's minds. Most Iraqis hope that their country can look forward to peace.

"One day everything will be different. I hope there will be a better future for my children."—*Abed*

Shaïmaa wants everything to be the same as it was before the wars.

Pronunciation Guide

Abed	**Ah**-bed		**Kebab**	Key-bob
Alia	Ah-lee-ah		**Kubba**	Coo-beh
Amira	Ah-mee-rah		**Kuwait**	Coo-wait
Baghdad	Bag-dad		**Mahdi**	Maw-dee
Falah	Faw-lah		**Saleh-Ali**	Saw-leh Ah-lee
			Shaïmaa	**Shaw**-ee-maw
Hala	Hah-lah		**Suher**	Soo-**air**
Hussein	Who-sane			
			Wasan	Wah-sun
Iraq	Ee-rock			
Iraqi	Ee-rock-ee			

Glossary

Academy A school for students, especially of music or art.

Civilian Someone who is not a soldier.

Independent Able to make your own choice about how to act.

Islam The religion founded by Muhammud. There are one billion Muslims in the world today.

Middle East The part of the world in which Iraq is situated. Other Middle Eastern countries include Egypt and Israel.

Mosque A building where Muslims gather together to pray.

Muslim A follower of the religion of Islam.

Republic A government in which all the members are elected.

United Nations (UN) A group made up of countries around the world, which works to bring peace and a better life for everyone.

Books to Read

Bratman, Fred. *War in the Persian Gulf* (Headlines). Ridgefield, CT: The Millbrook Press, 1991.

Deegan, Paul. *Saddam Hussein* (War in the Gulf). Edina, MN: Abdo & Daughters, 1991.

Hassiq, Susan M. *Iraq* (Cultures of the World). Tarrytown, NY: Marshall Cavendish, 1992.

Lerner Publications, Department of Geography Staff. *Iraq in Pictures* (Visual Geography). Minneapolis, MN: Lerner Group, 1992.

Index

Baghdad 4, 7, 8, 20, 21, 25

cars 19, 26
clothes 10, 26
currency 4

food 12, 15, 17
 kubba 12, 13, 16
 meat 12, 13, 15
 vegetables 12, 14, 15
 yogurt 12, 13

government 15

Hussein, Saddam 6, 10

income 5, 18

jobs 18–20

Koran 23, 26
Kuwait 6

language 4

music 21, 24, 28
 oudh 21

oil 6, 19

religion 4, 22, 26
 Islam 22
 mosque 26
 praying 26, 27

school 14, 18, 22, 28
 homework 9

television 5, 24, 25

United Nations (UN) 6
university 20

vacations 25

wars 13, 29
 Gulf War 28